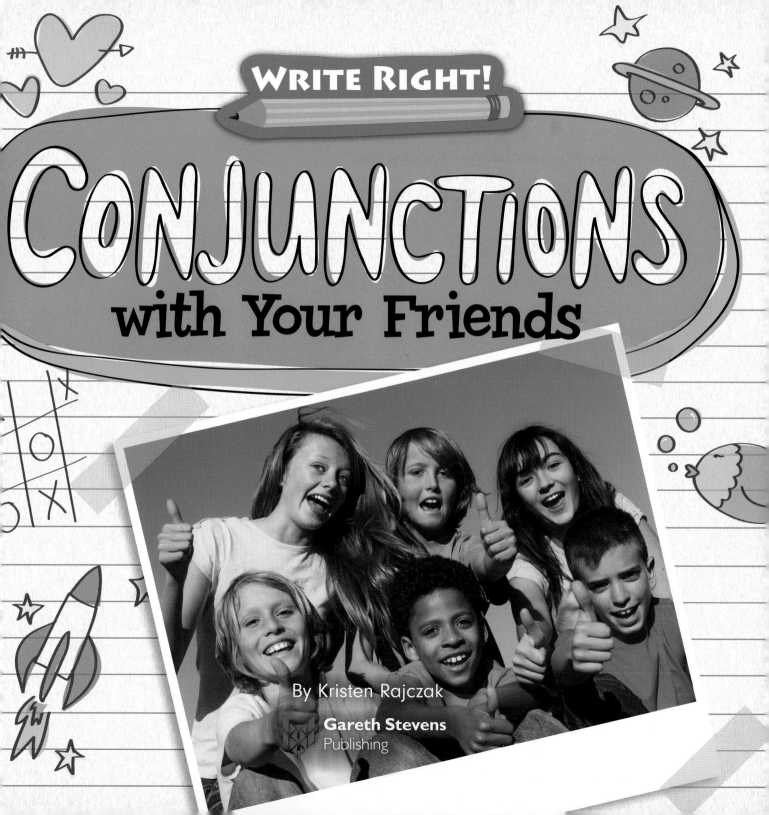

WRITE RIGHT!

CONJUNCTIONS
with Your Friends

By Kristen Rajczak

Gareth Stevens
Publishing

Please visit our website, www.garethstevens.com. For a free color catalog of all our high-quality books, call toll free 1-800-542-2595 or fax 1-877-542-2596.

Library of Congress Cataloging-in-Publication Data

Rajczak, Kristen.
Conjunctions with your friends / by Kristen Rajczak.
  p. cm. — (Write right)
Includes index.
ISBN 978-1-4339-9074-8 (pbk.)
ISBN 978-1-4339-9075-5 (6-pack)
ISBN 978-1-4339-9073-1 (library binding)
1. English language—Conjunctions—Juvenile literature. I. Rajczak, Kristen. II. Title.
PE1345.R35 2014
428.2—d23

First Edition

Published in 2014 by
Gareth Stevens Publishing
111 East 14th Street, Suite 349
New York, NY 10003

Copyright © 2014 Gareth Stevens Publishing

Designer: Sarah Liddell
Editor: Kristen Rajczak

Photo credits: Cover, p. 1 MONDY GODBEHEAR/Shutterstock.com; p. 5 Siri Stafford/Riser/ Getty Images; p. 7 KidStock/Blend Images/Getty Images; p. 9 © iStockphoto.com/kirin_photo; p. 11 © iStockphoto.com/Spotmatik; p. 13 altrendo images/Altrendo/Getty Images; p. 15 Arthur Tilley/Stone/Getty Images; p. 17 David Fischer/Digital Vision/Getty Images; p. 19 David De Lossy/ Photodisc/Getty Images; p. 21 NatUlrich/Shutterstock.com.

Printed in the United States of America

CPSIA compliance information: Batch #CS13GS: For further information contact Gareth Stevens, New York, New York at 1-800-542-2595.

CONTENTS

Words in the glossary appear in **bold** type the first time they are used in the text.

CONJUNCTION FUNCTION

Conjunctions are words that join parts of a sentence. They show the link between the parts. There are three main kinds of conjunctions:

- coordinating
- subordinating
- correlative

Before adding conjunctions, let's review what makes a complete sentence. A complete sentence has a main clause with a subject and **verb**.

Abigail plays soccer with her friends.

The subject is the **noun** doing the main action. That's Abigail. What's Abigail doing? She "plays"—that's the verb.

ON THE WRITE TRACK

A clause is a group of words with a subject and verb. A main, or independent, clause can stand on its own as a sentence. A dependent clause cannot.

JOIN LIKE ITEMS

"Coordinate" means "to act together." Coordinating conjunctions join words, clauses, or **phrases** to help them work as one unit. They connect two like things, such as two independent clauses or two verbs.

Three common coordinating conjunctions are **and**, **but**, and **or**. **And** joins similar items and is used to tell the reader more.

Sally **and** Frederick take swimming lessons.

T. J. asked Erik if he wanted to see a movie **and** have pizza afterward.

Lynette told Jean she would wash **and** return the shirt she borrowed.

When a conjunction joins two nouns that are both doing the main action of the sentence, the conjunction has created a compound subject.

THIS OR THAT

But joins **contrasting** items. It helps a writer show exceptions, too.

> Norelle is tall **but** doesn't play basketball.

> Pioter was supposed to meet Willy, **but** he felt sick.

> Everyone **but** Candice liked playing the video game.

Or joins **alternative** items. Use it to show the reader choices and possible outcomes.

> Josie wanted to have a pool party **or** a sleepover for her birthday.

> Selma **or** Gia would finish the race first.

> Should Rick wash the dishes **or** walk to the park?

ON THE WRITE TRACK

Other coordinating conjunctions include for, nor, yet, and so. Remember all seven by using their first letters to spell fanboys.

LINKING UP

A subordinating conjunction links a clause to the rest of a sentence. It always starts a dependent clause.

Some of the most common subordinating conjunctions are because, as, since, so, although, though, while, and after.

A subordinating conjunction may be placed between two clauses.

Mariana rode her bike, while Harry skateboarded.

In this example, the subordinating conjunction links the clauses below to show their relationship.

Mariana rode her bike.

Harry skateboarded.

ON THE WRITE TRACK

Sometimes, the subordinating conjunction is what makes a clause dependent. The clause may be independent if you take away the subordinating conjunction.

"Subordinate" means to "place at a lower rank." That makes sense, since a subordinating conjunction makes one clause dependent on another!

FROM THE START

Subordinating conjunctions can also start a sentence. Here's how it works!

Clause 1: Suri wanted to be Alyssa's friend.

Clause 2: She found Alyssa a bit bossy.

By adding **although** to clause 1, it becomes a dependent clause.

Although Suri wanted to be Alyssa's friend.

It needs clause 2—an independent clause—to be a complete sentence.

Although Suri wanted to be Alyssa's friend, she found Alyssa a bit bossy.

The subordinating conjunction links the clauses and makes the sentence's meaning clear.

ON THE WRITE TRACK

Dependent clauses act like a noun, **adjective**, or **adverb** in a sentence.

Bossy friends are like subordinating conjunctions—they can make you feel like you're a lower rank.

13

WORKING AS A TEAM

The final kind of conjunction may have two or more words that work together to link sentence parts. These are called correlative conjunctions. The examples below use some of the most common correlative conjunctions.

Both Alphonse **and** Dee needed to go to the mall.

They wanted **not only** to shop for school clothes **but also** to play at the new arcade.

A few hours later, Alphonse said they should **either** call his mom for a ride **or** take the city bus home.

ON THE WRITE TRACK

When you see a list of correlative conjunctions in a book, they are commonly written like this:

both...and
not only...but also
either...or

Proofread your sentence to be sure it makes sense. Reading it out loud is a good way to check!

15

KEEP THINGS PARALLEL

Using correlative conjunctions can be tricky! They join two parts of a sentence that should be treated equally. That means the word or words of the conjunction have to be followed by words or phrases with the same makeup. This is called parallel structure.

Take a look at the example from page 14.

They wanted **not only** to shop for school clothes **but also** to play at the new arcade.

Not only and **but also** are both followed by verb phrases.

ON THE WRITE TRACK

Often, writers can fix parallel structure problems by rearranging the words in a sentence.
Not parallel: Either Rita has to skip dance class or miss the school play.
Parallel: Rita has to either skip dance class or miss the school play.

If a verb phrase follows the correlative conjunctions, make sure the verbs are in the same form. So, if one verb is in the past **tense**, the other one should be, too.

17

COMMA USE

Commas separate two independent clauses linked by a conjunction.

Terri asked Kim to go skiing, **but** Kim had to visit her grandma.

A comma is used before or after a dependent clause that starts with a conjunction.

The group decided to go ice-skating, **though** it cost $5 to rent skates.

Since Rodney liked board games, Nathan taught him checkers.

ON THE WRITE TRACK

Commas separate three or more items in a series—and commonly come before the conjunction. Drew wanted to swim, play tennis, or read.

PUT THEM TO WORK

The paragraph below uses all three kinds of conjunctions. See how useful they can be when telling a story!

When Sidney woke up, the sun was shining, **and** the birds were chirping. She had big plans for her Saturday! **Both** Kendra **and** Hassan were coming to her house. Sidney couldn't wait to ask what they wanted to do. They could go swimming, ride their bikes, **or** play with her puppy! Sidney would let them decide, **because** Kendra and Hassan were her guests.

ON THE WRITE TRACK

Conjunctive adverbs similarly link ideas in a sentence. *However, moreover,* and *as a result* are examples of conjunctive adverbs.

COMMON CONJUNCTIONS

coordinating conjunctions	for, and, nor, but, or, yet, so
subordinating conjunctions	because, as, since, so, although, though, whereas, while, after
correlative conjunctions	both...and, not only...but also, either...or, not...but

GLOSSARY

adjective: a word that describes a noun

adverb: a word that describes a verb

alternative: offering a choice

contrasting: showing differences

noun: a person, place, or thing

phrase: a group of words

proofread: to read over and look for mistakes

tense: the form of a verb that tells the time of the action

verb: an action word

FOR MORE INFORMATION

BOOKS

Carter, Andrew. *Punctuation and Sentences.* New York, NY: Alphabet Soup, 2010.

Cleary, Brian P. *But and For, Yet and Nor: What Is a Conjunction?* Minneapolis, MN: Millbrook Press, 2010.

Fandel, Jennifer. *What Is a Conjunction?* North Mankato, MN: Capstone Press, 2013.

WEBSITES

Conjunctions
www.better-english.com/grammar/conjunctions.htm
Choose the correct conjunctions to complete these sentences.

Conjunctions and Connecting Words
englishwilleasy.com/word-must-know/conjunctions/list-of-conjunctions/
Use this website to review the many conjunctions and how they are used.

INDEX